The gods Psalms of the Bible & More

What Does the New American Bible (1970)
Have to Say about "the gods"?

by

Kathryn Sitterle

Published By:

Amoq (Hebrew Roots)

www.ThePublishedWord.com

Trade Paper Version ISBN: 978-1-964665-34-4

Hardback Version ISBN: 978-1-964665-35-1

Kindle Version ISBN: 978-1-964665-36-8

Printed on Demand in the U.S., the U.K., Australia, and the UAE

For worldwide distribution

Dedication

To the Lord of Hosts

Without Yah Sabaoth, this book would not have been possible. You are my All, and I love You with all my heart.

Contents

Introduction

I found the book, "*Hidden Prophecies in the Psalms*" written by the late J.R. Church to be very interesting. In it, he asserted that Psalm 1 had a message for 1901, Psalm 2 for 1902, and, so on, continuing this pattern. I was born in 1958, grew up attending a Catholic Church south of Pittsburgh, Pennsylvania, still had my St. Joseph's Catholic Bible, and wanted to know what Psalm 58 had to say for that year. I found that the first few verses of Psalm 58 say this:

"*Do you indeed pronounce justice, O gods; do you judge mortals fairly? No, you freely engage in crime; your hands dispense violence to the earth.*"

The New King James Version says it like this:

"*Do you indeed speak righteousness, you silent ones? Do you judge uprightly, O you sons of men? No, in the heart you work wickedness; you weigh out the violence of your hands in the earth.*"

I found three major stories of UFO sightings in 1958:

First, the front page of the *Lima Citizen*[2] on April 26, 1958, reported dozens of reputable citizens had spotted mysterious objects in the evening sky, including the Putnam County Civil Defense Chief and a trained skywatcher with the Ground Observer Corps.

Second, was a large set of UFO photos plus photo analysis and audio tapes with interviews of those who experienced UFO sightings in Brazil. (Many of these pictures have since been removed from the internet)

Third, a Monon Railroad train crew reported seeing a UFO in north central Indiana about 3:20 a.m. on Friday, October 3.[3]

A friend of mine talked me into purchasing a MacArthur Bible,[4] saying how lovely it was written, uplifting the reader. I was shocked to see the difference in the introductory verses of Psalm 58 between the St. Joseph Catholic Bible and the King James Bible.

I had heard on a television program several years before that our high-tech technology came from aliens, that it is an alien technology that we have in the United States today. This second Bible verse had me convinced that the statement I had heard on TV several years earlier was true.

I searched other psalms in the St. Joseph Catholic Bible to see if there were any other references to the gods. To my astonishment, there were more references to the gods in other psalms.

Psalm 82 is the next Psalm that mentions gods.

The heading is "The Downfall of Unjust Gods."

Psalm 82

God rises in the divine council, gives judgment in the midst of the gods. *"How long will you judge unjustly and favor the cause of the wicked? Defend the lowly and fatherless; render justice to the afflicted and needy. Rescue the lowly and poor; deliver them from the hand of the wicked."* *The gods neither know nor understand, wandering about in darkness, and all the world's foundations shake. I declare, "Gods though you be, offspring of the Most High all of you, yet like any mortal you shall die; like any prince you shall fall."* *Arise, O God, judge the earth, for yours are all the nations.*

Psalm 82

King James Version

¹ **God stands in the congregation of the mighty; he judgeth among the gods.**

² **How long will ye judge unjustly, and accept the persons of the wicked? Selah.**

³ **Defend the poor and fatherless: do justice to the afflicted and needy.**

⁴ **Deliver the poor and needy: rid them out of the hand of the wicked.**

⁵ **They know not, neither will they understand; they walk on in darkness: all the foundations of the earth are out of course.**

⁶ **I have said, Ye are gods; and all of you are children of the most High.**

⁷ **But ye shall die like men, and fall like one of the princes.**

⁸ **Arise, O God, judge the earth: for thou shalt inherit all nations.**

Psalm 86 is the next Psalm that mentions gods,

The heading is "Prayer in Time of Distress."

Psalm 86

*Hear me, L*ORD*, and answer me, for I am poor and oppressed. Preserve my life, for I am loyal; save your servant who trusts in you. You are my God; pity me, L*ORD*; to you I call all the day. Gladden the soul of your servant; to you, L*ORD*, I lift up my soul. L*ORD*, you are kind and forgiving, most loving to all who call on you. L*ORD*, hear my prayer; listen to my cry for help. In this time of trouble I call, for you will answer me.*

[8] *None among the gods can equal you, O Lord; nor can their deeds compare to yours.*

*All the nations you have made shall come to bow before you, L*ORD*, and give honor to your name. For you are great and do wonderous deeds; and you alone are God. Teach me, L*ORD *your way that I may walk in your truth, single-hearted and revering your name. I will praise you with all my heart, glorify your name forever, L*ORD *my God. Your love for me is great; you have rescued me from the depths of Sheol. O God, the arrogant have risen against me; a ruthless band has sought my life; to you they pay no heed. But you, L*ORD*, are a merciful and gracious God, slow to anger, most loving and true.*

Turn to me, have pity on me; give your strength to your servant; save this child of your handmaid. Give me a sign of your favor: make my enemies see, to their confusion, that you, LORD, help and comfort me.

Psalm 86:8

King James Version

⁸ **Among the gods there is none like unto thee, O LORD; neither are there any works like unto thy works**.

Since Psalm 86 is a long one and the other verses are very similar to the ones in the St. Joseph Catholic Bible (even verse 8 is very similar), I have quoted only this one verse.

Psalm 89 is the next Psalm that mentions gods,

The heading is "A Lament over God's Promises to David"

Psalm 89

*The promises of the L*ORD *I will sing forever, proclaim your loyalty through all ages. For you said, "My love is established forever; my loyalty will stand as long as the heavens. I have made a covenant with my chosen one; I have sworn to David my servant: I will make your dynasty stand forever and establish your throne through all ages." Selah ...*

*7 Who in the skies ranks with the L*ORD*? Who is like the L*ORD *among the gods?*

*A God dreaded in the council of the holy ones, greater and more awesome than all who sit there! L*ORD*, God of hosts, who is like you? Mighty L*ORD*, your loyalty is always present. You rule the raging sea; you still its swelling waves. You crushed Rahab with a mortal blow; your strong arm, scattered your foes. Yours are the heaven, yours the earth; you founded the world and everything in it.*

(There are almost 2 more pages of Psalm 89 to read.)

Psalm 89:7

King James Version

7 God is greatly to be feared in the assembly of the saints, and to be had in reverence by all those about him.

VS

7 Who in the skies ranks with the LORD? Who is like the LORD among the gods?

(St. Joseph Catholic Bible)

Psalm 95 is the next Psalm that mentions gods.

The heading is "A Call to Praise and Obedience."

Psalm 95

Come, let us sing joyfully to the Lord; cry out to the rock of our salvation. Let us greet him with a song of praise, joyfully sing out our psalms.

³ For the Lord is the great God, the great king over all gods.

Whose hand holds the depths of the earth; who owns the tops of the mountains. The sea and dry land belong to God, who made them, formed them by hand.

Enter, let us bow down in worship; let us kneel before the Lord who made us. For this is our God, whose people we are, God's well-tended flock.

Oh, that today you would hear his voice: Do not harden your hearts as at Meribah, as on the day of Massah in the desert. There your ancestors tested me; they tried me though they had seen my works. Forty years I loathed that generation; I said: "This people's heart goes astray; they do not know my ways." Therefore, I swore in my anger: "They shall never enter my rest."

Psalm 95

King James Version

³ *For the LORD is a great God, and a great King above all gods.*

vs

³ *For the LORD is the great God, the great king over all gods.*

(St. Joseph Catholic Bible)

Notice that the two versions are quite similar.

Psalm 96 is the next Psalm that mentions gods.

The heading is "God of the Universe."

Psalm 96

Sing to the LORD a new song; sing to the Lord, all the earth. Sing to the LORD, Bless his name; announce his salvation day after day. Tell God's glory among the nations; among all peoples, God's marvelous deeds.

[4] For great is the LORD and highly to be praised, to be feared above all gods,

[5] For the gods of the nations all do nothing, but the LORD made the heavens.

Splendor and power go before him; power and grandeur are in his holy place.

Give to the LORD, you families of nations, give to the LORD glory and might; give to the LORD the glory due his name.

Psalm 96

King James Version

⁴ *For the LORD is great, and greatly to be praised: he is to be feared above all gods.*

⁵ *For all the gods of the nations are idols: but the LORD made the heavens.*

vs

⁴ *For great is the LORD and highly to be praised, to be feared above all gods,*

⁵ *For the gods of the nations all do nothing, but the LORD made the heavens.*

(St. Joseph Catholic Bible)

Notice, again, that the two versions are similar.

Psalm 97 is the next Psalm that mentions gods.

The heading is "The Divine Ruler of All."

Psalm 97

The LORD is king; let the earth rejoice; let the many islands be glad. Cloud and darkness surround the LORD; justice and right are the foundation of his throne. Fire goes before him; everywhere it consumes the foes. Lightning illumines the world; the earth sees and trembles. The mountains melt like wax before the LORD, before the LORD of all the earth. The heavens proclaim God's justice; all peoples see his glory.

⁷ All who serve idols are put to shame, who glory in worthless things; all gods bow down before you. ...

⁹ You, LORD, are the Most High over all the earth, exalted far above all gods.

Psalm 97

King James Version

7-9 Confounded be all they that serve graven images, that boast themselves of idols: worship him, all ye gods. Zion heard, and was glad; and the daughters of Judah rejoiced because of thy judgments, O LORD. For thou, LORD, art high above all the earth; thou art exalted far above all gods.

vs

7 All who serve idols are put to shame, who glory in worthless things; all gods bow down before you. ...

9 You, LORD, are the Most High over all the earth, exalted far above all gods.

(St. Joseph Catholic Bible)

Now let's explore other verses in the Bibles that reference the gods:

Jeremiah 10:11

Thus shall you say of them: Let the gods that did not make heaven and earth perish from the earth, and from beneath these heavens!

St. Joseph Catholic Bible

Jeremiah 10:11

Thus, shall ye say unto them, The gods that have not made the heavens and the earth, even they shall perish from the earth, and from under these heavens.

King James Version

1 Corinthians 8:5-6

Indeed, even though there are so-called gods in heaven and on earth (there are, to be sure, many "gods" and many "lords") yet for us there is one God, the Father, from whom all things are and for whom we exist, and one Lord, Jesus Christ, through whom all things are and through whom we exist.

St. Joseph Catholic Bible

For though there be that are called gods, whether in heaven or in earth, (as there be gods many, and lords many,) but to us there is but one God, the Father, of whom are all things, and we in him; and one Lord Jesus Christ, by whom are all things, and we by him.

King James Version

Daniel 5:11

There is a man in your kingdom in whom is the spirit of the holy God; during the lifetime of your father he was seen to have brilliant knowledge and God-like wisdom. In fact, King Nebuchadnezzar, your father, made him chief.

St. Joseph Catholic Bible

There is a man in thy kingdom, in whom is the spirit of the holy God; and in the days of thy father light and understanding and wisdom, like the wisdom of the gods, was found in him; whom the king Nebuchadnezzar thy father made master.

King James Version

Exodus 15:11

Who is like to you among the gods, O Lord?

Who is like to you, magnificent in holiness? ... worker of wonders.

St. Joseph Catholic Bible

Who is like You, O Lord, among the gods? Who is like You, glorious in holiness, fearful in praises, doing wonders?

New King James Version

In ancient Greek mythology, Zeus was considered the most powerful and popular god, ruling as the king of the gods and the god of the sky, thunder, and lightning. He was considered to be the supreme deity in the Greek pantheon, residing on Mt. Olympus with the other major gods. He was known for his control over the weather, wielding the thunderbolt as a weapon and is depicted with a thunderbolt, a royal scepter, and an eagle, his primary symbols. He was seen as a protector of cities, homes, property, strangers, and guests, upholding justice and order. Zeus was referred to as "the father of the gods and men," signifying his authority and role as the ultimate ruler. In Rome, he was known as Jupiter.[5]

Endnotes

1. Oklahoma City, Oklahoma (Prophecy Publications: 1986).

2. The front page of the *Lima Citizen* (Lima, Ohio), April 26, 1958.

3. The Monroe County, Indiana History Center (https://monroehistory.org/2018/10/01/the-1958-monon-ufo-incident/)

4. The MacArthur Study Bible, New King James Version (NKJV) Copyright ©1998 by Reed Business Information, Inc. Study helps © Thomas Nelson, Nashville, Tennessee.

5. Information gleaned from Google.

www.ingramcontent.com/pod-product-compliance
Lightning Source LLC
Chambersburg PA
CBHW040857100426
42813CB00015B/2828